The Bob Sterry School of Burglary

*Essays, Poetry
and Short Stories*

The Bob Sterry School of Burglary

*Essays, Poetry
and Short Stories*

~

BOB STERRY

Sterry and Sterry, Publisher

to my late Father who was always
telling me to write a book

A poet is, before anything else, a person who is passionately in love with language.

W.H. Auden

We are cups, constantly and quietly being filled. The trick is, knowing how to tip ourselves over and let the beautiful stuff out.

Ray Bradbury

There have been great societies that did not use the wheel, but there have been no societies that did not tell stories.

Ursula K. LeGuin

Contents

Essays, Poetry and Short Stories

FOREWORD

Some years ago, Bob Sterry walked into the songwriter's open mic I host in Portland, Oregon, and had the audacity to get up and read poems. I was delighted. Songwriters need to be poets, and benefit from listening to poetry — especially, good poetry. Bob's poems are good, indeed.

Since then, I've had the pleasure of hearing Bob read many times. He and his wife Anne-Louise have become good friends of mine. They've joined me at a writing retreat in Donegal, Ireland, where I watched Bob still a pub with both poetry and song. His poems never fail to delight, with humor, insight, keen observation and a fine ear for language.

The poems, essays and one short story in this collection are accessible and fun to read, with depths of discernment just below their initial appeal. They entertain while provoking and rewarding contemplation.

"Yellow Pole Theater on the MAX" describes two groups of riders on a light rail train: one a couple with "their small child in his stroller," the woman "Wearing the basic scarf of her faith / A blue hijab"; the other "Scruffy, disheveled / Hauling a loaded four-wheel trailer." The poet's depictions of his fellow passengers along with his own reactions to them illuminate the depths that swirl, often unnoticed, beneath our most casual, everyday interactions. "A Tale of Two Picnics" juxtaposes a picnic at which "The bright sun's rays / Are dappled as they strike / The manicured greensward" with another that takes place on a "stony beach" where "the rain continues its attack," leaving the reader to ponder many possible interpretations: expectation versus actuality, subjective versus objective experience, class difference, etc.

Several pieces evoke the Pacific Northwest, particularly its climate and cycles of rain rising from and returning to the ocean. Not least, one of his essays includes good advice to the beer brewers of Portland, which I hope they will heed.

Over the years Bob has continued to uplift and entertain songwriters and poets alike with his poems — including at least one, I learned from this collection, that he wrote on the spot while awaiting his turn at our open mic. His work inspires us to hear the music in words and to tell simple truths with heart and humor.

The Bob Sterry School of Burglary is one of those rare treats that enriches while it entertains.

Matt Meighan
Portland, Oregon 2018

Acknowledgements

I cannot begin to thank my wife, Anne-Louise, enough for her encouragement and willingness to read and hear my work. Matt Meighan, I thank for allowing me to take the stage at Artichoke Music in Portland on many open mic. nights to read my poetry and urging me to keep doing so.

Blessings be upon my designer, Susan Bard, who has turned many documents into something beautiful. Thanks to Charlie Clark for guiding me through the intricacies of self-publishing. Barbara Bridge for her editing skill finding unneeded and needed punctuation and capitalizations. Thanks to Tom Hogan of the Milwaukie Poetry Series who has been writing and encouraging poetry for many years and was generous enough to review this book. Thanks to Oregon poet Emmett Wheatfall, and author Uvi Poznansky who were kind enough to write reviews.

And to the poets I never met but whose work inspired and gave me courage to write poetry; especially Billy Collins, John Betjeman, Charles Simic, D.H. Lawrence, Paul Violi, Barry Humphries, and A.B. (Banjo) Paterson. To too many authors, also unmet, of short stories and essays to list, but I will mention Saki (H.H. Munro), W. Somerset Maugham, Graham Greene, V.S. Pritchett, Ray Bradbury, and of course Oscar Wilde for laying a foundation in my mind.

INTRODUCTION

There is never a good time to publish another collection of poetry and essays. But then again, there is never a bad time to publish another collection of poems and essays. And so I feel entirely justified and motivated to add my own work to the mountain of words already bending the shelves of bookstores and libraries around the world.

In the spring of 2012 I put together a very short collection or chapbook of poetry titled *Wing Nut*. So called because instead of any traditional binding the pages were secured by a brass wing nut and bolt in the top left corner. Not elegant, hard to stack, but certainly unique, affordable, and curious enough to cause comment at poetry readings. This new collection of poems, essays and short stories contains a few of the pieces from *Wing Nut* and a selection of my work since then.

I am not capable of explaining exactly why poetry is important. It does not attract a lot of attention in our schools, and announcing that you are choosing to major in Poetry produces anxiety very high on the parental Richter scale. But it seems that poetry has not disappeared and the bookstores and libraries must make room for them.

Not quite so eschewed is the art of essay writing. But how many of us have been introduced to someone who calmly lets you know they are an essayist? Not even the famous journalists who write for *The New Yorker*, *Harpers* and *The Atlantic* will easily admit this. The essay. It was indeed one of the horrors of my own education; the fear of being instructed to write "an essay, three pages, single space, subject is dogs and their owners" to be marked out of ten by a cynical worn out chalk dusted English master.

I did not exactly choose my education and somehow became a chemist almost by default. I did not even start reading poetry until I was in my forties and actually daring to write any until my fifties. It was not until I larded my cabaret style singing show; another story; with poetry and saw the effect it can have on people that I began to read more of it and write more. Not exactly a power trip but a way of connecting perhaps.

The poems and essays in this collection do not have a theme although some are obviously very personal. I hope that they bring something to you or out of you. If you enjoy them I am doubly pleased.

Bob Sterry
August 2018

A Tale of Two Picnics

The bright sun's rays
Are dappled as they strike
The manicured greensward.
He, tall, lithe, teeth all aglow
In cream slacks and pastel blouson,
She, fair and fairylike in acres of shimmering gauze,
Alight from the auto
At the site of their 'manger al fresco'
Let us call them Justin and Jocelyn.
The basket is heavy
No matter.
He lifts it clear to carry
She gasps, he grins.
In minutes the scene is set
The rug, the plates, the glasses
The pate, the cold chicken,
The fruit … the wine.
He deflowers a bottle of Moselle,
Wishing it were her.
Guessing as much she blushes.
Ants retreat to nests
Wasps attack alternate targets
Flies zoom elsewhere to feed.
And all the while the sun
The golden sun continues to dapple.

The rain is not quite horizontal
As Joe and Judy
Run from the bus stop
To the stony beach.
Not quite horizontal
But driven off the sea it tastes salty.
He, ordinary, average, in a dampening grey mackintosh.
She, hair bleached, in a sister's frock and jacket
Holding hands,
And hold each a sandwich
Cellophane wrapped.
Squatting against the seawall
They eat.
Wet eyes flash bright signals.
Joe has a small thermos
It's vegetable soup,
And somehow a hardboiled egg appears,
To share.
The rain continues its attack.

The Bob Sterry School of Burglary

My first memory of streetlights was in a street that had very few. And the few that were there were gas lamps. The street was new in 1948. There were twenty or so brand new pre-fabs. Emergency housing designed to last a maximum of ten to fifteen years for people who had lost homes to the Luftwaffe during the Blitz and the later V1 and V2 rocket attacks. This included my parents who survived both of the latter. Many pre-fabs were still lived in at the turn of century.

When we moved in 1955 to another not so svelte neighborhood close to a satellite village of Sevenoaks in Kent the streetlights were much the same. A few spaced far apart and as before, gas powered. One of the lamps illuminated the telephone box at the top of the street where my Mother would go to enjoy every Wednesday or Thursday evening, after we had eaten, a five minute or less conversation with her sister Grace who lived twenty miles away. Often, she had to wait while one or two other people had made their calls and would stand in the cold with her precious coins in her hands.

The gas lamps eventually were replaced by electric standards. But whether gas or electric they all were extinguished at midnight and plunged the village and town into blackness. I loved it. It was a signal. As a teenager coming home from some adventure or other on foot, walking or running up the narrow lane toward home, trying to beat your curfew, and being suddenly without a shadow told you that you were in trouble. I had no wristwatch until I was nearly eighteen and depended on church and other public clocks to tell the time. Hearing those twelve chimes begin, and knowing that upon the last the streetlight would extinguish was a powerful signal.

Fast forward to the early seventies. My Mother finally could afford her own phone and sit on the stairs in our hallway and talk to sister Grace almost at will, but definitely according to budget. There were no 'free' calls. The streets were now lit by new sodium lamps. They did not go off at midnight and there was no real night anywhere anymore, and our village became an orange raceway for twenty-four-hour traffic. No longer could I stand in the middle of the road at the foot of the narrow lane, glance up at the church clock trying to make out the time in the comforting quiet and darkness. No longer could a young man experience that frisson of delight and horror at midnight. We now lived in continuous light. Lux Eterna of an unheavenly sort.

Which brings me to burglary.

When one asks why we have to illuminate our neighborhood streets with enough light that a jetliner could easily land on one, or one could easily read the very fine print in an insurance policy, the usual answer is "security!" There is this idea that thieves find illuminated premises unattractive targets for their work. As the President of the Bob Sterry School of Burglary, I say "Bollocks". Certainly, I could agree that a thief attempting to break into a well-lit house would find it embarrassing should he or she be discovered doing so by a passerby or a policeman. And so the obvious question becomes, at the usual hour when nocturnal break-ins occur where are these passersby and these lawmen? The odds against your being spotted as you pick a lock or force a doorway in a sodium light drenched street at 3:30 a.m. are large. The risks of not being able to find a lock to pick, a door to force, of tripping over a garden hose, a child's toy in the dark however are much higher. What better environment for a would-be thief than to work on a well-lit target, knowing that the police are unlikely to patrol your location for hours and that the neighborhood are all busy sleeping or glued to a screen behind the shades and unconcerned with the exterior.

And this is why, at the Bob Sterry School of Burglary, we focus our instruction on encountering both well and poorly lit targets and in general favor the well-lit variety. In fact, most of our graduates prefer to do their work in broad daylight so as not to interfere with their family life and sleep patterns. Night work is usually practiced by our more experienced and daring alumni who understand the value of light and the absence of urban, suburban and even rural surveillance.

And now I think back with wonder and amusement to those shadowed evenings when my heart would almost stop as the church clock struck the midnight hour and darkness enveloped me. If it is midnight as you read this please remember to extinguish your porch, deck, garage, and yard lights. After all, my graduates are about and seek the challenge of unlit booty.

Horizons are Deceptive

If I were an island on your horizon
And you a sudden ship on mine
What tension then begins
As we both speculate on intentions
As we both imagine consequences

If I were a ship on your horizon
And you a sudden island on mine
What tension then begins
As we both speculate on intentions
As we both imagine consequences

We are both island and ship
Anchored and free
Looking out and looking in
Looking for long journeys
Looking for escape from the same

We are both ship and island
Wandering and bound
Looking in and looking out
Looking for a strong safe harbor
Looking for escape from the same

Horizons are deceptive.

Love and Sunshine

You notice the browning leaves,
Early victims,
In midsummer
Late July and August
And they parallel our love
Crisping stale edges
Edging inward
Inward to where growing used to be
I blame the sun
The sun of truth
Blasting unmercifully on our greenness
And returning us to the soil
Of amorous compost.

Pinot

I met a girl named Pinot
She was blanc, she was gris, she was noir
In a sunlit Western tavern
To which I had wandered far.

When Pinot came to my table
And poured herself into a glass
I felt my senses burning
It was true love at last

She was sweet, she was dry, and frizzante
A bouquet redolent and fine
Tall, gold and full bodied
Her aftertaste...divine

But Pinot cannot linger
Longer than the glass
Our affaire was briefly intoxicating
Now part of my growing vinous past.

But into view comes Sauvignon
And the game begins again
So long as I have thirst
I doubt that it can end.

Sessio Cervisia, Ubi Es?

A recent article in *The Oregonian* about so called session beers caught my interest and has prompted me to set down my own thoughts on this volatile matter. You may be interested.

I reached drinking age in 1964. At that time where I lived in a sleepy commuter town some twenty miles south of London there were two pubs that were popular with teenagers and twenty somethings. Both served the thin, fizzy, metallic, skunky, pressurized chemical beer known as Keg Bitter. In the so-called swinging London sixties this fetid style brew had replaced many standard bitter beers as the main drink of the day. Not really even cheap and not cheerful. Imagine a yellow, slightly alcoholic soda water.

Americans do not know that in the UK most pubs were owned by the largest breweries. The managers or landlords of these pubs were told quite bluntly what to serve or be fired. There were so called 'free houses' around that served more traditional bitter, and whatever else they liked, but they were scarce on the ground in 1964. The big brewers had bought up all the best sites in the towns and villages.

In those wondrous days we young lads burped our way through thousands of gallons of this liquid muck until we finally discovered that there were actually beers around that had been brewed for a century or more. Bitters that had taste, character and history. These were in sharp contrast to keg bitter, whose only positive quality was that it was not very strong. Unless you were, as they used to say, "reely chuckin it dahn," it was hard to get drunk in the restrictive opening hours that pubs were allowed by law; 10:30 a.m. to 2:30 p.m. and 6 p.m. to 10:30 p.m. and wonder of wonders 11 p.m. on Friday and Saturday.

Many of the traditional bitter and other beers that had been almost killed off by the larger brewing companies had not only the aforementioned flavor and character but also had a range of strengths to satisfy the man or woman who was intent either on moderate or less moderate intoxication. There were beers that were tasty and satisfying yet with original gravities of less than 4%. They were most often called 'ordinary bitter.' And there were beers that had slightly higher original gravities; 4% and over; that were call 'best bitter' or sometimes 'special bitter.' And of course, there were hundreds upon hundreds of regional variations, which if things had not changed would have been slowly swallowed up by the largest brewing companies and would have disappeared forever. Some did, and some remain.

A sensible drinker would approach an evening out with his friends as theater. He or she had a few hours to create and enjoy the drama. What to do? Strategies varied but most common was to begin the evening with two or three pints of ordinary and see the night off with one pint of best. My own course was slightly different in that I would start with a pint of best to gain what I called cruising altitude before tapering to a slow landing with following pints of ordinary. At these gravities it would be hard to get drunk at this rate. And yet we felt we had enough alcohol.

In the early seventies I shared a ground floor flat with two other young men whose goals for any weekend could be simply summarized as 'beer and birds'. Our pursuit of 'birds' is another story for another time. But our pursuit of good beer prompted a serious campaign that involved a huge map of the city where we lived and surrounding countryside for a radius of about fifty miles. Upon this map we placed pins of various colors signifying pubs where not only could we find good beer but also felt welcome. The map was framed by old tickets to Rugby internationals, bills we intended to pay and some female undergarments that were a fixture of the flat irrespective of current renters. We called our work, 'The Survey.' And indeed, we worked hard at surveying good and bad pubs within our reach. It was often depressing to find that a good tip about a lovely little pub nestling by a river, with two bars, and amazingly rare, good food, served nothing but chemical brew, and could be described as locally ethnic (i.e. only locals welcome).

We were rescued by a superb development in consumer awareness — CAMRA, The Campaign for Real Ale. It was one of the most successful consumer campaigns ever effected. By promoting the presence of real ale as opposed to chemical brew and focusing on young and impressionable people CAMRA changed the brewing industry in the UK in less than fifteen years. It published a guide to real ale paid for by subscription that pointed out pubs where good beer could be had. Pubs started to try and get into the guide because they knew young people with disposable income read it. It is still very active today.

By the time I immigrated to the US in 1974 the real ale revolution was in full swing and we 'KNEW' where to go to get good beer.

Immigrating to the US I knew that I was losing something very dear to my social life. Good beer. In 1974 similar fetid chemical muck that had attempted to rule the British drinking public was the only thing that could be found in bars under the name of beer. I had a lot of friends who took me to many different drinking haunts in the NYC area telling me that this beer or other would be different. It was not. It was chemical lager through and through. Different labels but still thin, skunky, fizzy, and just awful. It was dreadful. And they had swallowed the same advertising hype that plagued the UK. "The Champagne of Beers," oh please! Rolling Rock, Steam Beer, Genesee Cream, Labatt's, Olympia, and worst of all Coors. Even less flavor than the rest! But so long as it was served ice cold so that one did not have to taste it, one could eventually get intoxicated. It was a sign of the times that another very plain metallic lager beer from Europe was considered exotic. Heineken. A Dutch Budweiser, but in a different bottle and imported. Imported…Oh boy!

And over the intervening years it has been a pleasure to watch the rise and growth of the American bitter. As an antidote for the barren desert years it is long overdue. I have spent way too much money going home to England just to get a decent pint. But there is this hiccup. There are in Portland, where I live now, many very creative and wonderful beers. Too bad their makers seem to think that the only marketing message they have is how flipping strong they are! It is a shame that I cannot drink over an evening without getting as my old drinking buddies used to say, legless. Over hopped, over strong and indigestible some of these beers leave me cold, and sometimes with a very odd aftertaste. A typical restaurant in SE Portland last week showed beer gravities ranging from 4.8% to 8.8%. There was a fruit flavored concoction that was marked 'girly' something, with a gravity of 3.3%. Fruit! No comment needed. We put fruit in certain beers to hide the flavor and make them palatable.

Think about this. Bars and restaurants in Portland can be open for many hours. People like to hang out in them for as many hours as they can. While there they may eat food at a much higher profit margin than beer. You need to keep these folk in the pub! So, a beer with moderate gravity and bags of character and 'reasonable' hopping is going to do that. It is called a session beer.

Portland brewers, come with me to London, and we will drink Young's ordinary and special. We will go to Henley and drink Brakspears, and on to East Anglia, once considered a wasteland of keg bitter, where we will try Adnams, and on and on. We will never get drunk, we will never be legless, we will taste good things and we will have had just enough. Just enough to make us happy, loquacious and with a sublime aftertaste. I am not suggesting you duplicate these beers here in Portland. You can't. And I'm not suggesting that there are no bad beers in the UK. There are a lot. Call me if you want names. But the basic style of a session beer is within your grasp and is needed now!

Do this and I will mention you in my will. Benediximus Portland!

Letting In

Night drives in as I touch the cat
Night gives two nickels for the cat and me
Night is coming anyway
Night always comes and surprises the cat and me
The cat and I are forgetful
The cat is glad to be in I guess
I'm tired of letting cats in
I'm tired of night being a surprise
I want the cat to say thank you
I want night to send a calling card
I want control of the animal and planetary world!

Monocular Malevolence

In the dark
Driving
Glance up to see
In the mirror
A following bulk
With a single head light
Its cyclopean beam
Is tracking me
Driving alone
On this dark route
And I shiver
In my seat
Sensing a monocular malevolence
Behind
Almost animal
A robo-creature
Stalking me in my tin box
For miles the lone yellow shaft
And its anonymous source
Sweep an unnamed fear into me
And when the road widens
And it passes me
I am genuinely surprised to see
That its driver has a head.

Tony's World

An improbable story of espionage

Tony was an ordinary Englishman. His parents were ordinary people. He grew up in an ordinary town not far from London and had ordinary thoughts. He was indistinguishable from his contemporaries. A reasonably well educated, reasonably well built, middle class Englishman with no particular ambition outside of getting a well-paying job. He was a sort of Home Counties Everyman.

It was in Tony's early twenties that the breakdown began. It was not the kind of breakdown that was particularly obvious to either his family or his friends. Perhaps breakdown is not an accurate description. But, slowly, over a period of several months a profound change in Tony's mind was fomenting. A series of fantasies and curious convictions were taking root. Family and friends noticed only a sometimes distracted affect, a glazing of the eyes at odd times. Whatever other delusions were swirling around his conscious and unconscious mind, Tony became more and more convinced of one particular idea. He knew instinctively that it was something that he could not, dare not share with anyone. And he never did.

Tony himself was not particularly aware that he was actually having a breakdown. He simply assumed that he was going through what every young Englishman had to endure at this time in their lives. He thought of it as a broadening of his life and perhaps his career. A career that up until then had been the rather mundane work of foreign exchange banking.

The idea that in addition to his work at the bank he was also employed by Her Majesty's Secret Service seemed to him quite normal and had always been so. Quite normal as well was the knowledge that he was not actually an active agent for the Queen, but being held ready, being prepared for future assignments; in fact, a 'sleeper.' A sleeper, an operative who wherever he may be is always awaiting a message to awaken to activate or reactivate him to begin or complete a covert mission. Tony believed this would come in the form of a telephone call. A telephone that would ring with a unique and urgent stridency, recognizable to him alone. He knew that there was no telling when this would come, or what he would be asked to do for Her Majesty's Secret Service. He did know that whatever else happened in his life from then on, he must be ready.

As everyone knows keeping secrets is almost second nature to Englishmen, and Tony kept his secret. He did not find it a strain. He continued his work at the bank and by and by was promoted not so much for his intelligence or quality of work but on the usual criteria that banks use, that of predictability and reliability.

What prompted the bank to send Tony to America to work in their New York office is unknown. After he left some of his colleagues in the London office were not sad to see him go, citing what they viewed as his annoying habit of staring at the telephone when supposedly talking to them. Tony himself toyed with the notion that his posting was part of his secret work and that he would be soon awoken.

In America, in New York, Tony enjoyed what many young Englishmen have experienced in that country and that city. The curious notion that Englishmen were somehow more interesting, mature and worldly than their American counterparts. He lived in a shared apartment with two other bank employees and they spent their non-working hours in a fairly tame pursuit of women and stock market tips. It was at a bank sponsored cocktail party, designed to impress new clients, that Tony was captured by Simone, the Personal Assistant to one of the ubiquitous bank Vice-Presidents.

Simone was a little older than Tony and much more experienced in many ways and easily swept Tony off his feet. She had of course seen him at the office and had been intrigued by his boyish Englishness and habit of gazing wistfully into space, or at telephones, which she interpreted as latent romanticism. Tony was not the only Englishman in the New York office. There were several working there in the European section, and Simone had examined them all, mostly from a safe distance. But she had decided that Tony was the one she wanted and the cocktail party was the perfect venue for his capture.

She was surprised by how easy it was, and in the taxi on the way to her apartment later that night found him very ready to be assimilated, as it were, more fully into American life. News of Simone's capture spread rapidly, and it was not long after that her Vice-President called Tony into his suite to discuss his future. He explained to Tony that if he was going to be 'enjoying' his P.A. regularly then the prospect of pillow talk concerning his particular client base and their various peccadillos had to be controlled. His solution to this was Machiavellian. He promoted Tony to his own staff as a Junior Vice-President. Simone was delighted and more pillow talk ensued.

For his part, Tony felt himself slightly outmaneuvered in a game he had not altogether anticipated. A serious development, but one which he could handle as a resourceful member of Her Majesty's Secret Service. After some thought he concluded that his mission would most likely be on American soil, and that events had been arranged for him to be placed in the right place, awaiting the right time. He saw his duty clearly and he and Simone were married fairly soon after his promotion to one of the executive floors.

Tony's habit of staring at telephones continued as he and Simone arranged their life together in the well-to-do suburbs of Westchester. It was not that Tony was especially good at his job but that he did not make any serious mistakes, and in the world of money it was enough to see him succeed. Simone was delighted. Delighted enough to let Tony know that she was going to have children. On the outside Tony made the correct noises and expressed his joy in the approved bank executive style. On the inside he grit his teeth at the prospect of maintaining a family which might put his secret mission in jeopardy. But on further thought he concluded that a standard American family was perhaps an ideal cover and relaxed his interior tension. Simone quit her position to become fully installed in the Westchester County social world.

The county social world was always ready to absorb bank executives, and Tony and Simone soon had the necessary club memberships to never have an open weekend to worry about, and an instant cabal of friends in all strengths. Once again, the curious allure of Englishness proved its worth, at least to Simone, who was able to rise in the club pecking order significantly faster than women with American husbands.

As time went by, as it must, Tony's interior conviction began to make itself harder to control. His until then intriguing habit of staring at telephones and gazing into space took more and more of his time. It began to irk Simone and even though the cabal rather liked this eccentricity in 'their Englishman' she more than once remarked to Tony that she wished he'd spend more time staring at her than the telephone. Swiftly aware that his cover was thinner than he wanted, Tony constructed a plausible explanation for his distractedness which he did not immediately reveal to Simone but kept in reserve. In the meantime he resolved to strengthen his cover in other ways, and they had their second child.

Even more time passed and Tony rose up the ladder of the bank hierarchy, reaching an exalted level where his eccentricities rather than setting him apart endeared him to his colleagues whose own unusual habits were well known to the company and were the daily nightmare of the Vice President of Personnel. His work now required much travel around the world and telephone calls at odd hours in the middle of the night from anxious bank employees in Tokyo, Tel Aviv and Mombasa often woke him and his family in Westchester. Tony installed two extra telephone lines in his home office, telling Simone and his children never to answer them or use them. They were for business only. One really was a service paid for by the bank which he used to take and make those nocturnal calls. The other was nothing of the sort. It was the telephone through which Tony knew he would be summoned by Her Majesty's Secret Service. With his cover thus reinforced Tony felt safe.

Nevertheless, Tony was not entirely in control of everything he did and from time to time Simone would find him sitting in his office staring at the special telephone. He would sit motionless for long minutes at a time unaware she was in the room watching, and even when she spoke he would turn his head only slowly and reluctantly toward her as if he were hypnotized by the handset. It sat in an area uncluttered by any of the usual paraphernalia a desk carries.

It was after a series of these incidents where Simone had come into his office, watched him for five or ten minutes as he watched the telephone and left without Tony being aware of her presence that she confronted him. Tony remembered his plausible explanation. He was growing tired of the bank and had put out discreet feelers to a much larger global enterprise. They had shown interest in him and promised he would be contacted by the president with possibly an offer that would far outstrip any counteroffer the bank might make. It was the chance of a lifetime he explained, and he had to be ready.

Simone chose to accept this, to her, implausible explanation with the acknowledgment that Tony must be under some severe strain at the bank. Indeed, recently he had looked weary and gaunt in a way she had not observed before. And she also recalled the behavior of her own father and uncles, who often buried themselves in their dens, workshops and lodges, constructing separate and parallel lives away from wives and children. Making a simple addition of Tony's eccentricity to these patterns and her conclusion of executive stress she resolved to let it pass, also remarking to herself that a nice upswing in income would not be hard to take. It would certainly do her no harm at the club, where the pecking order was always in flux.

What neither she nor Tony could explain was how long it would take before such a dramatic career change would actually happen. Months passed with Tony spending more and more time alone in his office; watching. As is often the case, it is children who notice things more acutely than adults, and Tony's were no exception. It was his daughter who one day remarked to Simone that although one of the phones in Daddy's office was always ringing the other one never had. Once more Simone confronted Tony. And again, he vigorously defended his diligence, adding that he was doing this for the family and if they would show a little more patience it would be rewarded.

Even in the almost zoologically varied environs of the executive floor Tony began to stand out and not in a favorable way. It was not that his work was suffering. It was as it had been for decades, impeccable, unremarkable, but necessary. But, just as he had done at his home office, Tony spent much time sitting alone watching one of the telephones on his desk, where it too sat in an uncluttered area. That might have been ignored if it were not for his insistence on having entire days in his schedule that were not available to not only clients and other executives but to the President of the bank himself. Even the previously judged most eccentric inhabitants of the executive floor toed the line when the President requested their presence or service and effected a simulacrum of normalcy. Tony's commitment to Her Majesty's Secret Service, in his mind at least, superseded any other, even a Captain of American commerce.

Tony saw his cover beginning to fray and flailed around for more solid shelter. But he was as he had always been, an ordinary Englishman, with an ordinary imagination which did not help. Nevertheless, his resolve and conviction that he would one day be activated did not waver. Despite now having waited for nearly twenty years for his call he felt more and more convinced that his time would come. The call would come by the telephone with a unique, strident and urgent ring. His faith in the service dwelt in the core of his being like a rock and directed his life. A life which observed from the outside was becoming increasingly bizarre. Acceptable eccentricity gave way to whispered asides and rumors. Not just at home and the office but at the club where it did not help Simone and her concern with club pecking order.

No one quite knew what happened the day Tony lost his grip on the pretense of normalcy. It began with an ordinary day in the life of the bank, an ordinary day in the comfortable bosky avenues of Westchester. Even in Tony's house an inexplicable calm had settled. It was one of the night cleaners who discovered him. Slumped in his leather Vice President's chair, an empty cup of coffee hanging from his right hand. The cleaner, who was actually a graduate of John Hopkins Medical School working to pay off some debt in the summer vacation, confirmed that Tony was very much alive but needed the ambulance he had immediately called.

Thanks to the very expensive medical plan enjoyed by bank executives Tony was diagnosed within the hour at Mount Sinai Medical Center as having endured and survived a moderately severe brain aneurism. Thanks to his obscenely high, but bank paid, insurance premiums not only his life but his mind seemed to have been saved. Simone and the children rushed to the hospital and found Tony awake and alert. Tony stayed in the care of some of the best nursing staff money can buy for two weeks while they established he was ready to go home and resume his quotidian life.

Simone drove Tony home on a hot August afternoon to the house they both called home. The hallway and his office were full of flowers and cards from the bank, the club, neighbors and clients all over the world. His children ran to him and smothered him with kisses and hugs. It was Hollywood in Westchester.

Later that evening Tony felt strong enough to step into his office and make an early start on recovering his professional momentum. As he sunk into his chair and began to pick through the cards and files that couriers had delivered over the past week, his eyes rested on the telephone, the special telephone, now almost covered in good wishes in paper and petals. He did not immediately understand or recognize it and was unsure why it was there. The air conditioning hummed on and on and Tony was staring at the telephone but did not know why. Reasoning that he had just come through a life threatening experience and could not be expected to see everything clearly so soon he left the room and went to bed.

In the following days Tony made several attempts to do some work for the bank. He sat at his desk in his house and from time to time his eyes rested again on the telephone. He reached over and picked it up. A dial tone. No giveaway message waiting dial tone. Nothing.

It was Simone who one day soon after his return came into his office and found him once more staring at the telephone. It was too much. For a long five minutes she circled him and his desk berating him for the various indignities she had been made to suffer at the club, for his secrecy, the loss of time with his children, his unwillingness to share whatever it was he was expecting to be announced via the telephone, with her his wife and it all focused on the telephone.

Tony looked first at the telephone and then at Simone and told her that he had no idea what this telephone was for and why it was in his house. Simone looked first at Tony and then at the telephone and exploded into a further but shorter tirade which let Tony know almost to the hour exactly how much of his life he had dedicated to staring at it and his explanation of why. The episode exhausted them both and nothing more was said that day.

A few days later Tony made the journey into the office where a lukewarm reception greeted him. A brief interview with the President let him know that his position at the bank was secure and he should resume his work full time as soon as possible with the proviso that he correct some of his more disturbing behaviors. Tony was confused, but readily agreed. What behaviors he thought to himself and resolved not to ask the President but one of his own equals on the executive floor, or better still one of the Personal Assistants whose access to the corporate cortex was likely to be more accurate and up to date.

And so, after a few days of casual inquiries, Tony was able to piece by piece form a picture of himself before the aneurism and did not recognize it. At least not at first. Not at first. But slowly like an inadequately weighted corpse thrown into a pond, it all came to the surface of his consciousness. The telephone watching, the gazing into space, the hermitic reluctance to set a schedule, and just as slowly the cause, the base, the reasoning that fueled it all floated up to confront him in gradual shadows of recollection.

On the train home that evening, sitting in the club car with men just like him, Tony attempted to make sense of it and concluded there was no train journey long enough. Simone, as usual, picked him up, and they went to the club for dinner. News of Tony's 'normal' health issue; executive aneurisms where not quite commonplace but easily forgiven; had quickly reached the cabal and Simone's position in the pecking order was, as it were, on hold, and she and Tony were allowed their usual table overlooking the putting green. Nothing apart from ordering their food and drink was discussed, but a tautness of speech and atmosphere lingered over the embroidered linen and embossed cutlery.

Arriving home, Tony felt it necessary to go to his office and once again make some headway on the backlog his illness had caused. The sight of the special telephone triggered the earlier recollections and suddenly he saw the decades of his life so far spread out to view and he could not bear it. In the space of a minute he realized that he had squandered years, decades of his life pursuing a fantasy, an impossible fantasy, that he a very ordinary man was somehow to become an agent of Her Majesty's

Secret Service on a mission of importance to his country. In the same minute he realized that he was now actually free from that delusion but not free from the damage it had caused, and it was this new burden that then made him insane, or close to it.

Tony sat at his desk, crying, and it was there that Simone found him, cradled him in her arms for a while before taking him to bed.

When Tony awoke the following morning he was a broken man. Not so broken that he could not still put on a show of normalcy at the office. Not so broken that he could not make conversation at the club. But the spark was gone. And as he performed this charade of correct or normal behavior his work actually began to deteriorate. Tony was not a star banker, and after a short consult with the corporate lawyers the President decided it would be relatively easy to persuade him to retire with grace and promote one of the younger men already eager to take his place. One less nightmare for the Vice President of Personnel.

Tony had not the mental strength to fight either the bank's decision or a need to survive. Apart from his now destroyed delusion the bank had been nearly everything to him, and while understanding the bank's need to clean house and restore confidence, the loss of both and having neglected his family, his children, Tony felt left with little to fight or live for. His own mind had betrayed him and only a coincidental medical emergency had allowed him to see the truth.

Tony did not take long to die. He did not take his own life in an easily recognizable way, but he did over the space of a few years fade away. The severance package offered by the bank was generous enough to allow Tony and Simone to stay in their home. Tony tried to work as an independent consultant, advising smaller financial institutions on foreign trade, which had been his niche. It failed to stop his mind constantly reviewing the past. There are not many who can acknowledge in full the waste of their lives, and Tony was not among them. Day by day, every damn day, the reality of his delusion weighed upon him mentally and physically. He became a shell. After few not so successful contracts with a network of Indonesian export companies a particularly virulent flu virus turned into pneumonia, against which Tony had little or no ability to fight and he died at the ridiculously young age of fifty-five.

Tony's funeral was attended by all those who had assiduously neglected him in the years after leaving the bank, a few remote relatives who had made the trip from England, and a sort of cotillion of ladies from the club and their reluctant husbands. Large wreathes from the President of the bank and the Vice president of Personnel were prominent if not somehow ironic.

The usual platitudes echoed along with asides about how Tony often seemed distracted. But the overall impression was of a man who contributed the average requirement. An ordinary man. Simone and the children seemed sad but almost relieved to see the last of Tony.

Simone particularly felt that she had in some way been deceived by him. Life for her would be a lot easier now. The life insurance policy she had insisted upon years ago paid in full and at the club there was a special soft spot for executive widows, and Simone was able to keep the table overlooking the putting green; at least for a while.

Simone had arranged for the funeral reception to be catered at the house. As the guests tucked into the smoked salmon and cheese platter, and downed the not so reasonably priced Chardonnay, Simone's head suddenly snapped in the direction of Tony's office. Its door was firmly shut. But from inside the closed office came the unmistakable sound of a telephone ringing. And it rang with a unique and urgent stridency. High above Broad Street in the office Tony once called his own, another telephone was ringing with a unique and urgent stridency.

Cricket

You think I don't see the stars
You think I don't wonder at the sky
As I crouch here
Unseen
Unseen but heard
A small chirruping twig of chitin.
I am come quickly to this world
And leave the same
I have some purpose
Which is not to entertain
Or become a romantic icon of your late summer sentiment
I am here solely to exist for a brief moment of beauty
I dare you to claim more.

London Road

That short wispy haired lady
Fighting her way against the wind
Up the London Road
Is my Mother.
Lips pursed she is returning
From the hairdressers, the post office
And has yet to pick up steak and kidney
For the pie she will make
For the boy who is coming home
For her son who will soon be there
For the man who loves the pie
For her child who loves her.
Her lips are pursed in determination
Against all the obstacles
Real and imagined that stalk her.
Lately that climb past the church
Made her puff.
Tiredness, her weakened heart
Struggling to keep up.
Perhaps the thought of another winter
Another wet and windy struggle
Up and down the village
Up and down the London Road.

Discretely her body decided
To give up.
No more struggling
No more tiredness
No more puffing and halting
For my shy timid Mother.
No more making tea
No more cleaning
No more washing
No more worrying
For my Mum.
Her three sons
Middle-aged and modern
Stand miserably with their Father
Standing in suits in the municipal crematorium.
Rain and wind, my Mother's enemies
Howl and lash outside
Lost without their old victim
Inside aging relatives
Exchange scared glances
Wondering who is next.

We Don't Eat Scandinavians!

Sometime in the late 1950's and halfway through the Sunday roast pork dinner my Brussels sprouts are mixing nicely with the fresh apple sauce, crackling and a curious mixture of mashed swede, potato and margarine that my Mother often produces as part of this meal. It is a moment to relish in any English schoolboy's meal. Still plenty of good stuff left on the plate, and the promise of apple pie for dessert, or 'afters' as we called it. And even before we get to the pie there is also a likely fight for my Father's leftovers. He often does not finish what he has on his plate and seems to enjoy watching his three sons jockey for an extra portion whilst my Mother tut-tuts her disapproval of this crude display. But she is outnumbered.

And in case you are wondering, no, we were not cannibals, and did not eat people from Scandinavian countries, however tastily prepared. However, Swede, or Swedish Turnip or what Americans call Rutabaga was and still is a frequent part of my diet, and a recent article in the Food Day section of *The Oregonian,* which while not disrespectful of this fragrant and nutritious vegetable, was not as fulsome as it deserves, and prompted me to do a little more research into 'brassica napobrassica.'

I had barely touched the keys and I discovered that in Ithaca, New York, every December there is an International Rutabaga Curling Championship, and closer to home the Advanced Rutabaga Studies Institute in Forest Grove, Oregon. The Wikipedia entry for the Rutabaga let me know, amongst many fascinating pieces of information, that the preparation served by my dear Mother so long ago is called, in Scotland, 'clapshot;' a delicious schoolboy term. "More Clapshot for you, dear? It contains 42% of your daily requirement of Vitamin C!"

From the *Wikipedia* entry I discovered the physiological reason why many people find Rutabaga intolerably bitter. Poor dears, they are cursed with especial sensitivity to the glucosinolates which it contains, as do watercress, mustard greens, turnip, broccoli and horseradish. It is in their DNA. Nothing can be done. Nothing can be done except invent recipes that attenuate or mute that characteristic; which brings me by a circuitous route to a recipe which does just that. I have been making 'quattro radice purea' since I was introduced to it at a relative's Thankgiving Dinner some twenty years ago. Their version contained Parsnip, Turnip, and two other mystery roots neither of which were Rutabaga. My version, of course, is a nostalgic nod and homage to my Mother's unwitting Clapshot, and contains constantly variable proportions of the following:

- The flesh of baked Potato (keep the skins!)
- Roasted Onions
- Roasted Rutabaga (or Swedish Turnip)
- Roasted Turnip
- Roasted Parsnip
- Roasted Carrot

...all mashed and blended with butter, salt, pepper and occasionally Parmesan cheese, and then baked in a casserole, or stuff the potato skins and bake.

Of course you have counted the ingredients and are questioning my mathematics. But before you get too critical let's just go through them. A Potato is a seed tuber, a Rutabaga is a swollen stem. Turnips, Parsnips and Carrots are roots and the Onion is a bulb. So, perhaps I should call the dish "Purea di Sei Verdure?"

No matter, it is delicious, nutritious, a wonderful conversation point and economic.

My Personal Fruit Fly

It is September and my personal fruit fly has returned
From his long vacation,
And is happily perched on the rim of my wine glass
Politely hopping off whenever I reach for a sip,
Quietly resuming his place when I set down my glass.

I can hardly resent his microscopic intrusion
Especially when I find that he and a partner have ended
Their wandering chitinous lives
And are now jointly denting the meniscus of my economy
    class Chardonnay.

Smoke

It felt like a thousand years of smoke
had burnt my mouth
When the slender woman spoke.
She smoldered on my mind
And burst in flame one day
With the wind of lust
With the oxygen of love
Seared me body and soul.
But lust is always fleeting
And the ashes of love are stone cold.

Rhubarb

I learned about Oxalic Acid
At seventeen
When less than anxious for yet more information
More notes on a chalkboard
In a malodorous Sulphurous school room.
Hastily copied in pencil
Scribbled then and required to be transformed
Later, into copperplate, almost textbook pages.
To be judged as adequate; or not.

Oxalic Acid; not as deadly.
But in a close league,
To the clear deadly liquids
Held in the dusty skull marked bottles
Within easy reach of any manic schoolboy.
Dusty bottles in a rack
In a rack on a bench
On a bench where I sat
Where I sat wondering why my mind
My sharp juvenile mind would never grasp
Molecular Valence Theory quite as well

As the taste of a girl's lips
The smell of her hair
The ring of her laugh
The answer to a question in her eyes.
Years later
When that girl had gone
I read that Oxalic Acid is found in Rhubarb leaves.
Pie making always brings such fascinating memories.

Peenemunde

I was looking up Peenemunde on the Internet this morning. I was interested in finding the exact location of a place I have known existed for a very long time. It sits on a small island in the Baltic off the North Coast of what was once the German Democratic Republic; or as many knew it; East Germany.

I was doing this on Memorial Day because on this day and November the 11th, Armistice Day, I do remember. The task of remembering is not without some challenges for me. I lost no one in any war, police action, or peace keeping exercise, or whatever you like to call occasions when young people die for reasons that they may not altogether understand. I have little personal connection with any of this. Growing up in Post War England, I knew that the War was the last thing anyone wanted to talk about. It was still with us in rationing (until 1953) bombed out buildings and damaged people. But all my family wanted to do was get on with life and get away from the horror.

My Father was very annoyed by anything that told what he thought was a lie about the war. And there were many around. He did not like the cartoon portrayals of brave and rugged British Tommies killing fleeing hideously stereotyped Nazis that I read in my copies of British schoolboy weeklies. He did not like the endless stream of jingoistic and nationalistic American and British movies that flooded the movie screens. He thought war was foolish and told me to beware of any nationalism that crept into my way of life.

He was not a pacifist and would have killed anyone who harmed my Mother or me and my brothers. And he was clear that the second war had to be fought. But he would not tolerate my brothers and me saying that the Germans, Japanese and Italians were all evil monsters. Even when we were old enough to be aware of the horrors of the concentration camps in Europe and Asia and found our credulity stretched he implied that we could not fully understand the enormity of this unless we had been there. Unless we had been Germans, unless we had been Jews, or Japanese or anyone who had to make choices in the face of an unrelenting tyranny. He did not care for Germans or any other race. But he did not believe in the moral superiority of any one race or nation over any other, and now neither do I.

And later when I came to know what my own people had done to other races around the world, in distant lands and as close as Ireland, I found it easier to comprehend my own flawed nature. And even later when I discovered that the very Elementary School I attended in my village was named after an 18th century general part of whose fame rested on his strategic distribution of disease laden blankets to Native Americans in the fond hope that they would die. Then I too became more and more averse to nationalism; anyone's nationalism.

And so, on this day in spring, and on November 11th, I put out a flag and give a lot of thought to the millions of men and women who died mostly unnecessarily because some warped and genuinely evil men and their dubious nationalism got out of control. I feel a deep sadness, and almost a sense of fatalism when I read the rhetoric published in our own newspapers and blasted across the internet and broadcast media, and on this day whose purpose is now nearly almost forgotten by a large proportion of the population I feel doubly affected.

It was in the last years of the second war that my parents, having already endured the blitz, were bombed out of two apartments in succession. In the first case by a V-1, or doodlebug, and in the second by a V-2. Both attacks did nothing to change my Fathers outlook. His only comment to me about the rocket attacks was regret that a fine pinstripe suit he had bought recently using many precious clothing ration coupons had been lost in the debris of one of them.

Both rocket weapons were developed and tested at Peenemunde by teams of scientists and engineers headed by Werner Von Braun, who went on to do many things in a different country. My Father and Von Braun never met. I wonder if my Father would have asked him for a new suit.

May is National Grilled Cheese Sandwich and Poetry Month

Soft curdled interior now at its eutectic
Holds a bifurcated square of gluten
Equally carbonized together
In an orgy of ill-advised but sensual nutrition

Maxwell's Axe

Maxwell's axe is not as famous as his silver hammer
But properly used it cuts through existential claptrap
Faster than Wittgenstein's even less famous poker.

Yellow Pole Theater on the MAX*

Episode One

I smiled at them
And their small child in his stroller
Only the man smiled back
Climbing aboard the southbound MAX
Clinging to the yellow poles
Framed by the yellow poles
In a transit theater.
She did not smile
Wearing the basic scarf of her faith
A blue hijab
She would not smile
And my smile
Meant to acknowledge
Our short common journey,
And something warmer
Appears a threat.
She could not smile
At a stranger.
Only a fixed grimace
Anxiety or fear
Lay on her face
Eyes flicking left and right
And to her child
Obliviously squirming.
Our cultures lay between us
Surely not an impervious barrier

*The MAX is Portland, Oregon's light rail system

Episode Two

I did not smile at them
Climbing aboard the southbound MAX
Clinging to the yellow poles
Framed by the yellow poles
In a transit theater.
They did not smile at me.
Scruffy, disheveled
Hauling a loaded four-wheel trailer
Presumably their lives
And for ten minutes
I guessed the content of those lives
The sad decline
The erosion of resources
The flight of friends
The flight of hope
But when she
Bulky, purple hair, pushed in face
Pulled out an IPad
And then he
A scarecrow in near rags
Pulled out an IPhone
I had to guess again.
Modern poverty
No less humiliating.
Our economies lay between us
Surely not an impervious barrier.

The Yellow Pole Theater
Never fails to play
Never fails to jolt me out of
My assumptions and my complacency.

Unused Wings

Working under a cloud of sadness
Cleaning a mother's home
After their death.
All the familiar objects
Are so much heavier
Loaded with emotion
Triggered by every trinket touched.
And the unfamiliar
Items never seen before
Not really secret
But secretive
Shed an unfamiliar light
Or a tragic one
On the lost life.

Add some desire you had
For resolution
Or proof of affection
A letter un-mailed, explaining…
Everything, less,
Or adding further mysteries.
Photos signed with a revealing scrawl
In a curious masculine hand.
And flowing in your mind
As you reduce a life to a list
For disposal, dispersal
A certainty

A knowing
That what you see is not the whole
The whole life

There's something missing
That might explain
Her wistful expression
Her unexpressed longing,
The aura of regret,
You recall it easily.
A perfume of disappointment
Lingering.

And when you finally
Discover her dark journals
Her writing, but reflecting a stranger
A talent, a power, a presence
Never revealed, never known
But rich and sharp
With bright witty language
You understand this is a set of wings
Dusty with neglect
Heavy with melancholia
Unused wings.

Unused wings
One pair out of millions.

Le Grande Festival des Grenouilles Cuites

A few years ago, I accepted an invitation to a Frogmore Stew Party in late May. I am told this is a South Carolinian Low Country dish. It reminded me immediately of a little known and possibly fictitious event in France. Here is a reminder from a citizen of France ….

"Of course, I hope you all know that this date is probably coincidental with Le Grande Festival des Grenouilles Cuites which occurs every year in the small town of Mangezvite, nestled in the rustic foothills of the Massif Centrale. Every late May and early June tens of thousands of frogs have from time immemorial gathered along the banks of the short rapidly flowing streams that descend from the Massif into the Rhone Valley to feed on the abundant insect life and of course mate, vigorously and often. It is this public and erotic display that persuaded the historical inhabitants of the region to create some of the best recipes for Frog known to man and celebrate this in a festival of amphibian love and gustatory excess. Young and old alike delight in donning the traditional Robe Longue de l'Amour de Grenouille and hop around in lustful leaps hoping to show that they are Le Grand Vert de Mangezvite. The Mayor of Mangezvite chooses the best dressed female frog and receives special favors from the winner in a sort of Droites de la Grenouille Aînée. This old practice has been banned many times by the authorities but no one takes any notice, least of all the Mayor. Visitors from Lyon, Clermont Ferrand and even from Paris have often tried to attend the Festival but the mayor does not announce the exact date and time until the signs are right. Any visitors who do show up are encouraged to stay and be fleeced by the local hoteliers and restaurant owners who then publish their new Menu de Grenouille. C'est tres cher! No-one really knows exactly how many years the festival has been running but the town prospers, even if all the children do seem to look terribly similar to the mayor."

My Medical Inventory
or Erectile is not my only Dysfunction

Scanning from the ground upward over my torso
Reveals a disturbing inventory of dysfunction and decay
Brachymetatarsia, in both feet!
Asymmetrical leg length
Reconditioned knees
Atrophied right quadriceps
Misbehaving Piriformis
Nocturnal micturition insomnia
Hernia scar
New! appendectomy scar
L4 & L5 Vertebrae way too chummy.
Epicondylitis, right side.
Are these breasts? Are these jowls?
A score or more of epithelial polyps decorate my neck and torso
Gum recession
Moderate gastro intestinal reflux disease
Likely causing persistent Rhinitis.
Three diopter challenge in both eyes
Slightly relieved by cataract surgery
Dermatochalasis, left and right
Somewhat corrected by Blepharoplasty
Scintillating Scotoma (look it up!)
Finally, to cap it all...Androgenic Alopecia
With rear solar panel developing.
And yet when asked
I reply, Oh, I'm fine! I'm fine.
And you, and you, still love me.

Kerosene Kettles

There are four giant kerosene kettles
Tied to the wings
Of the machine
In which I sit.
Voices speak in the air
Confident and bland.
The owner of one of the voices
Sets fire to the kettles
And the whole machine leaps
Into the air
Me with it.
We all pretend it's OK
And sit quietly
Until the voices speak again
And tell us
The fire is out
And we can leave
Into a strange city
Or home.

Ocean Kinetics

The sun
The irresistible sun
Has stripped off a thin slice of the ocean
Hoicked it high in the sky
Less fish and salt
Dragged it over my house
Dragged it over your house
In Oregon
Where it lies
A leaden blanket
Shielding us from the same sun
And from time to time falling
Falling to escape
Through streams and rivers
To escape into the ocean
And once again
The sun
The irresistible sun
Will return it to you.

The Moon is Leaving

The Moon is leaving …
She's had enough of us.
She won't illuminate our love scenes any more
No more moon in June
A singer to croon
To a saccharine tune
While we fools spoon
We mad apes.

Not so suddenly
She saw our hate
Our lust for power
The scarcity of our compassion
The famine of our love
The gross abundance of our falsity
And will leave us dark, and tide less
For more rewarding and gentler orbits.

Asked to stay
She softly reminds us
Of the millennia in which we failed
Failed over and over
To hear her soft song
Were deaf to love
So deaf, and
Chose the songs of Mars.

Asked to stay
With tears and anguish at our loss
With loudest promises of change
With the loudest promises of change
She softly reminds us of earlier compacts
Broken, over and again,
And sings of her patience
Her long soft patience
Now exhausted.

The moon is leaving
She's had enough of us
She's had enough
Enough …
Of the mad ape.

That Sucks!

I had not been in the United States very long before I heard new and creative ways to insult someone with whom you may have serious issues. In the fall of 1973 I was working in a bar in Union City, New Jersey. The job required me to dress in a scratchy polyester imitation monk's habit. My shift started at 7 p.m. and finished when the place closed at around 2 a.m. In those hours I would serve wine, onion soup and cheese platters to the not so sophisticated clientele sitting on hard wooden seats in what pretended to be a monk's wine cellar; an imitation of an original venture in New York City. Among my rough and ready customers was a rotund red headed American Irishman, Dave. Dave was intrigued with the first Englishman he had ever met in the flesh. He took me under his wing in a strictly unofficial way and introduced me to some fascinating bars on Tonnelle Avenue in Jersey City and North Bergen, and more on Second Avenue in New York City. Chinatown was also part of his introduction to food and much drinking in the NY Metro area and we often ate there around 3:30 a.m. after my shift. It was only twenty minutes away from the bar via the Holland Tunnel.

It was during our transit to one of these dining experiences that I heard the first of many new-to-my-ears American insults. Dave had a flamboyant driving style that involved a lot of loud shouting to any other driver he judged lacking in his level of skill. Most of this shouting took place in the safety of his car, a beat up Ford Galaxie of indeterminate vintage. On this occasion however he actually rolled down his window to pass on his advice and commentary more clearly to a pedestrian who thought it was safe to cross Canal Street at the same time Dave was using it to get to 21 Mott Street where our favorite restaurant, Hop Kee Club 66, was waiting for us. Dave began the dialogue saying, "Hey, Mother F****r! where in hell are you goin'?" An equally inflammatory response was returned rapidly to which Dave replied, "... and your Mother Sucks Elephants!" in a tone and volume he was sure would clinch the exchange in his favor. I could see that the unlucky pedestrian was genuinely insulted and began walking in a menacing way toward the car to continue the conversation physically. Dave solved this new development by flooring the gas and we shot off toward our dinner. I was mightily interested and over our fried oysters quizzed Dave on the etymology of the phrase. Dave's command of the English language was sketchy at best and involved a lot of grunting and stock phrases. For example; to express indifference Dave would growl, "The f*** I care!" To show contempt he would hiss "f*****g ass-hole" and so on. And so it took a while to find that the new insult was meant to imply that the receiver's Mother was such a low life, such an awful human being, that she would even fellate pachyderms. Over the Moo Goo Gai Pan I also discovered that there were alternate abbreviated forms, e.g. "Ya Motha sucks" and "You suck!" It was obvious to me that this insult should be limited in use to mostly impolite male company, and so it proved.

It was with a shock some twenty years later that I found the phrase, "That Sucks" being used by high school friends of my children, and probably my children too behind my back. Did they know the likely source, the probable etymology of the phrase they used to express not so much a revolting insult but an opinion on unfavorable circumstances? Did they know anything of the pachydermic connection and the deviant, not to mention impossible sexual practice from which this seemingly harmless comment could have been derived?

The Elephants are saying nothing.

Singing Terracotta Pot

Small persistent African Violet
In a tacky green plastic pot
Needed something grander, I thought
To encourage it, from now on.

I cleaned up a terracotta pot
Found in the garage.
Which as I was rinsing off the older dirt
Sang a song to me.

Noise like steam, but not steam,
Escaping from a tiny radiator
Singing of nothing I knew
Kept me fascinated at the sink.

Small violet now sits in terracotta.
Larger accommodation, fresh soil
Placed in the warm laundry room to resettle
Will you now sing a duet of color for me?

Vernal Equinox

The vernal equinox
Is cold as midwinter
And even though the sun
Is passing over the equator
Heading North to our tropic
And the birds, the noisy birds
Ring my ears with their enthusiasm
Our river is swollen
And the western Cascade slopes
Remain white on the clear-cuts
When I glimpse them
Through the grey curtain
That is tearing the pink blossoms
Off annually optimistic Cherry trees.

Oregon Spring

It's the contrast that stuns
So green, so green
Against the low grey clouds
Of an Oregon spring
As deciduous leaves lighten
The evergreen backdrop.
But the sky reflects an earlier month
When the low grey and soaking clouds
Hung over the curbside coffee drinkers
Pretending that forty-five is sixty-five
Degrees.

At Solstice

At solstice
Our fiery helium warrior
Takes his bow at Cancer
And turns southward
While winter grins at Capricorn
Girding her frigid loins
To turn northward
With icy relish.
In three moons
These two pass
Without a nod at equinox
Both intent to scorch or chill
Alternate tropics.

New Year's Day

An approximate calendarial construction
Not like the solstice, which is fixed, planetary, or even
     galactic
At the instant of the solstice our tired helium warrior
     begins to find it in himself to regain his former
     strength
Day by day a few more lingering minutes of faltering
     illumination bless a darkened landscape.
And even if the thermal mood remains frigid and
     forbidding
And the Pacific Ocean extends a somber blanket across
     our skies,
Our hearts slowly rise and acknowledge a hope that is
     always there.
These are days to get through in the Pacific Northwest.
No bright frosty Currier and Ives New England scenes
     for us;
Only the dull leaden weight of an aerial ocean hanging
     always on the verge of falling.
We find our path to brighter times,
Still moist, with games and jokes that acknowledge
     the drippy truth
And point either forward to the dry time or relish the
     other side of rain …
The good side.

Our forests, rivers and fields are superlatives of their kind
    and feed hungrily this dark wet time to stay that way.
I glimpsed our tired warrior today,
peering wanly between folds of the suspended ocean
looking for his old burning fields.
I raised my hand in salute to the force I know that rules
    my days,
though masked and muted a while he will as ever burn us
    once more.

Hands Up Everyone Who Knows and Loves the Negroni!

In a summer long ago, but it was called 1968, I was bored enough one lunchtime to sit and listen to a man in a pub tell me some nonsense. Pubs, of course, are and hopefully will always be constructed at least partly for the transfer of nonsense from one wannabe character to another. So the setting was right. And the particular pub, The Black Boy, had always been well stocked with wannabes. So the extras cast for my short drama were appropriate.

This man who was roughly my own age had the slight advantage over me of actually having a career at that moment. Whilst I was a soon-to-be failed Chemistry student carrying only the price of one pint of what passed for beer in that pub in my jeans, he was a Purser of some modest level in the Merchant Navy with more than ten pounds sterling in cash upon his person! He was not in uniform; I was.

He was bored, as homecoming seamen often are. Returning to their rural or suburban hometown to find that the local nightlife, not to mention the vacuum of daylight hours, does not quite match that of Caracas, Buenos Aries, Monte Carlo, or even Fort Lauderdale, they become impatient to get back to their ship, and pass their leave hanging around the saloon bars of pubs and golf clubs, hoping to find someone to talk to who would have even the remotest idea of what they had seen or experienced.

As it happened I actually had a friend who was also in the Merchant Navy, and was also a Purser, for the Cunard Line, and so knew something of this man's life before he even opened his mouth. And in a further coincidence I knew this man's older sister and had fancied her awfully a few years before this incident.

He was not much of a storyteller, and far from being fascinated by his revelations of shipboard shenanigans, beach parties with American girls of a certain *type*, how much money he made, and what his long term plans were, I fast become as bored as he already was.

But he did buy me drinks. And since I had been brought up as a polite young man I felt it rude to snub the man. It was within half an hour of closing time; English pubs closed at 2;30 p.m. in those days; that he suggested we have a Negroni. It may have been a desperate move on his part to regain what he may have perceived as my wandering attention, or it may have been a desire on his part to get as drunk as he could before the pub did actually close.

Up until this time my experience of cocktails was limited to the Gin and Tonic, and a taste of a Whiskey and Ginger (what my dear old Aunt Edna called a Whiskey Mac).

It took quite lot of cajoling by my new acquaintance to get the barman to agree to mix Gin, Vermouth, and

Campari together in equal parts, and find a suitable glass into which he could pour the concoction. And then there was an awkward moment as he calculated the price. But the barman was as intrigued as I was and once the price was settled he set about his task with enthusiasm. Economically it was the single most expensive drink I had ever enjoyed. And enjoy it I did. It was fabulous! Bitter, sweet, fruity and cool, consuming all the ice the pub had.

The pub closed and I wandered off to the bus station to catch a bus home. I must have stunk. Getting off the bus at my village a girl I hardly knew stopped me to say how much she liked my sunglasses. I had forgotten that I was wearing any.

Roughly 39 years later I sat at a roof top bar in a hotel in Naples close to the train station with my youngest brother. He'd never had a Negroni. The bartender here was adept at correcting this shortage in his experience, and we had two before setting off to find a restaurant for dinner amongst the piles of garbage that decorate the streets of that dense and fragrant city.

Fraction

A photographer stands
Shutter cable in hand.
An image is beating
On his camera door
Not demanding entrance
Light, energy is indifferent
But continually present
And changing.
He thinks he saw something
His machine can capture
On a thin reactive pellicule.
But chemistry only keeps
A part of the whole
Pulsing available spectrum,
And the image emerging
Later in a darkened room
Is, of course,
A fraction.

Let's Demo!

Sometime in the middle sixties I was a failing student at one of the shining towers of Britain's technological revolution. I was failing for two reasons. Maybe three. I had chosen the wrong discipline. Chemistry instead of Art. The college was in Brighton. I had gotten myself elected Vice President of the student union.

I lived in a boarding house run by two irritable and thoroughly obnoxious Germans, or were they Austrian or even Swiss? My room was a closet on the third floor. It was freezing, even in September, and the scratching noises at night were not made by other students attending to their acne. Luckily the student I had shared rooms with in the previous year was also living there. Luckily, I say because he had a motorbike. It was a Matchless 350. A big step up from his earlier ride, a puny Triumph Tiger Cub. And it was on this bike that we rode the four or so miles out of town to the shining tower to continue our chemical studies. On the days when our schedules did not align I had to walk a mile to a bus stop and spend valuable beer money on a ticket. I got off at a stop right in front of the college. Remember this bus stop.

I do not remember the exact date when the foreign student fee issue came to our attention in the union office. The union office was a festering tip, but for the section where the one permanent administrative employee, provided by the college, sat with a typewriter and duplicating machine awaiting our instructions. She was a mature woman. She saw all and knew all. In her fastidious corner all was order. Nothing much happened in the union office except when the LP that was currently playing had to be replaced or re-cued so that silence should never creep into the student lounge where many future champions of Britain's techno-fury studied or mostly played cards while trying to drink appalling vending machine soup and coffee, or worse digest the unusual offerings from the refectory. Orders were placed with the brewery to restock the bar which opened at 5 p.m., and the captains of the various sports clubs came in to claim their team travel allowances and use the one phone line to call either the captain of that week's opposing team, or their mothers or their girlfriends. The big project for the union was organization of the Charity Rag Week in the fall of each year. Then and only then was there a semblance of activity in the office. But more of that another time.

Whatever the exact date was is not important. What was important was the ego of our Union President who had been casting about for an issue to make his name in local and national student politics. And it was he who at one Union Meeting dropped the news on us that the Government of the day was going to radically increase the fees of foreign students studying in the UK. He raved at and lambasted the fools of Whitehall and their cruel injustice that would quite plainly cripple the development of the ex-colonial countries from which these students mostly came. The student committee took input from all quarters and since we were nice middle-class lads with a healthy (sic) guilt about our nation's colonial history we too felt indignation rising and made motions to be voted on and the results sent to the holy of holies, the National Union of Students (NUS). And when our colleagues at a famous University only a few miles further up the road decided to go to London to join a demonstration being organized by the NUS to take place on the very steps of Parliament we felt we had no choice but to do the same.

And so, it was one dreary dark winter day that the President, the Treasurer, the Student Secretary and myself, the Vice President, set off in the Treasurer's mini car; he was well-to-do; and drove up to London to set things right. It was a dreary ride and parking in London was a nightmare, even then. In a large hall we listened to the tirades of our NUS leadership and certain politicians who perhaps had taken a liking to the cause based on the number of immigrant citizens in their constituencies. Suitably fired up we marched off to Parliament where we were kept in check and off the road by mounted Police (two or maybe three). We shouted in our polite English way for a little while and then went home thoroughly disappointed that no one had asked us any questions, and the police had been overwhelmingly nice and considerate of our right to be there, and not one M.P. had deigned to interrupt his or her lunch to see what the noise was all about. I have no idea how many demonstrators there were but less than two thousand I would guess. It was an anticlimax.

The return journey in the tiny metal box that was the Treasurer's car was gloomy except for the proximity of the Student Secretary's knee to mine and her hand which I held and stroked in a way I thought was sure to excite. Arriving back at the shining tower we went straightaway to the bar where the President uncharacteristically bought us all a half pint of beer. We continued to rail and plot and pass motions condemning the government as they refined their plans to discriminate and punish our overseas friends.

And it was these friends that not so subtly attenuated the indignation and fervor that I possessed on this issue. Our college in its short two-year history had managed to attract a large number of foreign students. Nigerians, Ghanaians, and Malaysians. Indeed, I played Field Hockey with several brilliant Malaysians. It was a huge Mercedes full of these friends whose rapid passage by the bus stop where I was waiting (I told you to remember it) caused a bow wave of water from a large puddle to wash over me as they left college for the day to return to the rather nice hotel where they were all staying for the whole year at their countries' expense. I was left standing, soaked and chilled, and with a new perspective on many things.

A Walk

I met life one day
Walking along
And life joined me to talk.
For years we walked,
Together.
It was fine, my life.
And later,
When I stumbled
Life would slow down,
Waiting for me.
Now I stumble more
And life waits even longer,
So that I wonder when
Finally,
Life will turn and say,
"I can wait no longer"
Striding onwards.
Then I will have a new and darker companion
Who does not walk with me, or ahead,
But silently behind.

Who was there always
Some distance
Unseen around a corner of perception.
But now I have to see,
And I find myself
Picking up the pace
To stay ahead
Ahead of that dark silent figure
Who will, one day, cover me
With an inescapable shadow.

Yellow Cords

At Artichoke Music on Hawthorne Avenue in Portland, my adopted city, there is every other Thursday a songwriters' roundup. A simple open mic where local and visiting musicians can get up and try out a new song. It is a lovely, warm and welcoming place. The sound system is good, the lights flattering and the beer and wine are reasonable. It is a listening room, not a bar with music. People actually sit still and listen to the players. And on some evenings there is extraordinary music when the muse strikes one of the regulars or an out of town wiz takes the stage and lets it go. For the $5 entrance it is a bargain.

Sadly, the lease is up for the 'Choke. The whole of Hawthorne Ave is being slowly redeveloped, boutiqued, in that hideous boxy, sterile style that local architects are foisting on us. In the same building as the 'Choke is Crossroads Music, a funky vinyl emporium. And the 'Choke shares the parking lot with Cubo, a sweet little Cuban food joint. So, the 'Choke is moving to another part of town and will never be the same.

I started to go because my wife and musical partner became part of the scene there, and one songwriter's roundup I got up and read one of my poems. I loved it. And after all, what is a songwriter but a poet with music. At least twice I have read poems that I actually wrote while sitting there listening. The deal at the 'Choke is this.

You pay your $5 and if you want to play you write your name on a slip of paper and leave it in a basket on the bar. The MC shuffles the slips, plays an opening song, and reads off the first three players. It can be a long wait and folk often leave at the break and the last player thanks everyone for opening the gig for him and sings to the holdouts.

I write my poems from prompts or ideas I have written in my notebook or fingered into my cell phone. And so it was last week that I had placed my slip in the basket and realized I had nothing to read. Nada. Zip. Zero. Zilch. I had not even brought my notebook with me! On the table in front of me there was an announcement for one of the 'Choke's workshops. Its reverse side was blank. Perfect. On my cell phone some weeks ago I had entered the words 'yellow cords', remembering how much I had lusted after a pair of yellow corduroy pants long ago in unaffordable, trendy, hip, mod, Carnaby Street, London. The epicenter of cool clothes for the swinging sixties. Like all clothes in London, it was way out of reach for students like me. While the first three players were doing their thing on stage I wrote this poem and after the break read it to a bemused audience who had no idea where Carnaby Street is or what it was in those far distant days.

I always wanted yellow cords
Since I saw them in a movie in 1965
Yellow cords
With a purple shirt
And a white man's afro.

I had the 'fro ... then
Really...
Not now.
And I am truly over purple.
But yellow cords, man!
Deep creamy dreamy yellow cords.
Blue shirt
Sky blue linen shirt.
And red shoes, red shoes, yeah!
Fifty years ago in Carnaby Street
Trendy spendy hip clothing London street
Fifty years ago in Carnaby Street.
But...
Forty years in the corporate suit
Can do a number on you,
And yellow cords had to wait
For no GOOD reason
And for no GOOD reason I remain
Cordless, yellow-wise.
But I did get the red shoes
Oh yeah, dammit, I got the red shoes
Red-Suede-Chukka-Boots.
On line, ninety bucks,
*Carnaby Street, eat your f*****g heart out!*

It could use a little editing, which I may get to. I have to admit on reading it to the crowd I felt a sort of relief. As if I had been bottling up resentment against that street and its pretentiousness for all those years. Well, I wonder who or what is next?

Going to Cairo

I thought it would be more romantic than this.
I thought it would strangle me with its strangeness
Walk up to me with a sword in its oriental mouth
And bump into me,
Jolting me out of my occidental seat into the stinking dust
    of the gutters.
I thought the Mohammed Ali mosque would wrestle me
    to the ground with its shocking bare immenseness.
I thought my nostrils would burn with the assault
    of unnamed spice.
I thought my ears would crumble with the muezzins
    call at noon,
When all the dogs in Cairo enter a canine Koran reading
    contest.
I thought the pyramids would crush me with too much
    history and indifference
I thought the city of the dead would turn my gut over in
    its emptiness and blank windows
I thought the Nile would bewitch me and turn my
    blue blazer to Joseph's coat
I thought Tutankhamen's chariot would run over me
I thought so much and I thought so much
That it brought me here where I would not be except
    for Cairo
For Cairo was a poetic enema
And purged some foolishness from me.
She lightened my load
And with her sister Bombay
Will always be on my cerebral medicine shelf
To take in case of cabin fever.

Basil Wars

Ever since I first tasted and then devoured my first Tomato, Basil and Mozzarella salad, splashed with olive oil and a thimbleful of vinegar, I have tried to grow at least the first two ingredients in my own yard. More competent and confident growers will say with pride "my garden". It is not through any misplaced sense of agricultural modesty that I eschew the word, more a realization that my ignorance of things growing will always exceed my tiny knowledge; and the real area under cultivation is an always an otherwise weedy corner haphazardly laid out. Harvests, however pleasing or bountiful, surprise me. Perhaps I should rejoice that I can still wonder that the shriveled-up fragments I buried in the cold earth long ago could cause this mass of green.

My first tomato harvest in New Jersey in 1977 was a revelation. I had never grown anything but juvenile skin outbreaks until that time, and when I weighed one of the red darlings at over one and a half pounds I was damned for ever to be an irregular grower. And that is what I have remained. I really don't think I have learned very much about growing tomatoes in the intervening years and harvests. I did have a lot of fun.

It wasn't until 1984 that I grew my first Basil down the side of the garage of my second house in New Jersey. It did not seem to need much attention; it grew easily and full, even on the east side of the building. No pests seemed to worry it, and my capricious watering habits only seemed to encourage growth. The memory of the marvelous pleasure of my first homegrown Tomato, Basil and Mozzarella salad can never pall.

It took me a year to find out how different things are here in Oregon. I was deceived by the summer of '94. In May of that bright year I set out my usual messy mix of Beefsteaks, Roma, Better Boys, and Early Girls on the clay bound soil of my new home. The Sun shone with gorgeous continuity all summer; I watered and watched. And just as before nature returned in full measure and more my disordered effort. My new freezer became stuffed with the prize of my diligence in rich red puree. It was then that I remembered with a sudden feeling of loss those halcyon salads and determined that next year I would enjoy that pleasure once more.

With a lovely and misplaced sense of anticipation I bought six heavily fragrant Basil seedlings and set them out in a moderately sunny spot next to the Oregano, Mint and Lemon Balm. I suppose I must have thought that the cheers I heard were from some local sporting event instead of from the United Gastropod Local 52 (Herb Committee) who had been wondering up until that time when was I going to set out something for them to destroy. Now I was restoring their faith in humans who had, as they believed, always set out such a smorgasbord of plant delicacies around this time of year that Local 52 always referred to May as Christmas. They set to with their usual efficiency and diligence, and within forty-eight hours had rid my yard of nearly half of my delicate Basil plants.

My sense of betrayal was not softened in any way by their eschewing the Mint and Oregano. Out of the very soil that feeds the fragrant delight of Basil comes this treacherous bag of goo to suckle. Bait I bought in big bags. To no avail. Surrounding my precious green darlings with a cordon of death from Home Depot Garden Dept. seemed only to arouse a terrifying esprit de corps amongst the slugs, and they flung themselves in ever increasing numbers at the barrier in a gastropodic parody of King Henry's assault on the French at Harfleur, when he appeals, according to Will Shakespeare, to his weary and desperate soldiery … "Once more unto the breach, dear friends, once more; or close the wall up with our one footed dead!" New battalions slid up over the silvery glistening remains of their dissolved brothers. I began to see my fondly remembered salad as King Arthur beheld the Holy Grail; very distantly.

With the wounds of '95 still fresh in my memory I set out to make, in 1996, a more calculated defense of the precious Basil. Once more I bought the tender and aromatic seedlings. But this year I planted them not next to the Mint and Lemon Balm, growing wildly thank you, but in long planters in the warmth and security of my own laundry room.

Reassuringly the tiny green leaves grew with succulent good health under my un-ironed shirts, next to the three months supply of Graham Crackers and Woolite. My anguish on the morning when once more I found the undeniable evidence of the predations of a basil munching goo bag, was a low, low point in my horticultural life. How, I wondered, had a slug become so charged with sense of purpose that it had dared to enter my house to fulfill its revolting and heartbreaking digestive mission? As before I put out bait and waited. Further raids were made, and I began to despair. I saw myself actually buying bunches of Basil in a supermarket, carefully hiding them under my cereal and cold cuts, blushing violently with shame when the clerk yells out for a "price check on Basil!"

It was not until the day after the next that mounting the stairs from my basement office to prepare lunch that I spied my enemy doing the same. Just as I was on my way to the refrigerator from the basement, this mucilaginous murderer was on it's way from a container of seemingly inert potting soil, crossing the Formica desert, to the Basil Buffet by the window. Even as I drew near and watched with fascination the monster gripped the base of the planter and waving its knobby antenna as if asking for a no-smoking seat, set off toward the luscious green leaves. Speechless with a mixture of horror and admiration I gazed on, hypnotized by the grim determination shown by this slick black envelope. In a dog or a horse it would have brought cheers and tears. In this case a quick grab with the pasta tongs, a short step to the powder room and …that's what good plumbing is for folks … my nemesis temporarily defeated.

But are we safe? If our potting soil is contaminated can the end of civilization be too far behind? And when will I taste again the glory of a Tomato, Basil and Mozzarella Salad?

A Little Taste of Tarmac

A Poem written by my neglected bicycle

A little taste of tarmac, Bobby
Let me spin my wheels
A little taste of the long flat road
I've forgotten how it feels

A little taste of tarmac, Bobby
Make my chainwheel hum
A little taste of the up hill grind
Thirty miles and some

A little taste of tarmac, Bobby
Way out among the farms
A little taste of dust on your lips
My metal soul would calm

Climb up onto the saddle, Bobby
Clip into the pedals tight
Feel my frame respond to you
You always crank me right

Stay with me in the saddle, Bobby
Our ride will be as sweet
As the wash of lactic acid
From your shoulders to your feet

It's good with you on my saddle, Bobby
I know you feel the same
You push my pedals hard now
And laughing call my name

Lean easy in those corners, Bobby
Accelerating the while
My frame is all aglow now
On your face I sense a smile

Flying home with you, Bobby
You get the adrenaline kick
It makes you sprint the last half mile
And smooth out the left hand flick

A little taste of tarmac, Bobby
I am waiting stem unbowed
Come find me soon and ride me
Before my rims corrode

A little taste of tarmac, Bobby
Make me spin my wheels
A little taste of any road
Or forget how good it feels.

A Fine Vocabulary
or An Entertaining Fool

He was equipped with a fine vocabulary
Far in excess of his intellectual needs
An entertaining fool
Stocked with dictionaries
Obscure constructions
Medieval verbs
Circumlocutory, verbose
Impenetrable.
A simple mind hid amongst
A confusion of entangled phrases
As if using a foreign language
Assembling hopefully meaningful phrases
Where a listener may find coherence
A simple message.
Every request
Every Statement
Observation
From his mouth, no matter how mundane
Appeared decorated
Embellished, almost…
Baroque

In this wordy fog
It was hard to know
Hard to find
Traces of a real person
A tangible, relatable identity
Something predictable.
In the swirling wind of
Constantly shifting
Complex expressions
Seeming riddles.

He was a prisoner
A lifer
Doomed to remain
Incarcerated in his usage
Dense, cloying, exaggerated, unyielding
Usage he could not avoid.
Unconscious, reflexive, merciless usage
He did not struggle,
That ended long ago.

Sibling Trees
or The Lonely Ones

We know these places
Anonymous acres of asphalt
Laid for our convenience
Laid for our conveyances
Laid for our tin box convoys
Marked for our convenience
Marked for our conveyances
Marked for our precious tin boxes
We know them
We hate them
We use them
And over and over again we
Use and know and hate them.
And on the perimeter
On the furthest edge of convenience
Over on the grubby rubbly lip of retail development
Or there, along a strip of garbage strewn curbstone
Among the cans, butts and condoms,
Are the lonely ones
Five, or six or seven … lonely ones.
An architect's afterthought

A landscaper's two hour shift
A nurseryman's profit
A planner's nod to some notion of beauty
A cynical wave at ideas of balance
A cheap wink at nature …
Five or six or seven thin lonely trees
Missing their forested brothers and sisters
Siblings they never knew and never will
Standing here now … for us
And it doesn't work.

*Some years ago I attended a Halloween party dressed
in a sinister black cape and wizard's hat.
I was accompanied by three ugly witches. We called
ourselves 'Dunsinane Associates' and this was
our corporate brochure ...*

~

Dunsinane Associates
Modern Witchcraft for Modern Clients

ש † ‡

~ ALL THE BENEFITS OF THE ANCIENT ARTS

WITHOUT THE SMELL AND GUILT ~

WITCHCRAFT HAS BEEN LARGELY OVERLOOKED in today's Modern World. Overlooked, discarded and abandoned in favor of the seeming efficiencies of technology and logical thought. This is especially true in the world of business. Companies that once secretly or openly resorted to the use of a tax deductible malicious service have gradually changed tactics and now almost wholly rely on what may be called good luck. The profession of

Witchcraft has to assume much of the blame for this. It refused to move with the times; insisting on retaining its frankly rather nasty and smelly uniform; employing only the ugliest candidates for its top positions and ignoring all the basics of customer service and support.

Dunsinane Associates is the first Dark Arts company to become fully integrated into modern business. Recognizing that in the moral sense nothing has changed in the business community led to the conclusion that a high quality and responsive malicious service with an understanding of 21st century business systems would be a very desirable commodity.

Taking on **Dunsinane Associates** as your dark partner will almost immediately set your company on a different plane on the road to success. Our customized spells and curses put you in the driver's seat when it comes to an unseen advantage. We have spent many centuries perfecting all our best and most potent formulations, recipes, curses, spells and maledictions.

We enjoy a very high success rate and retain customers by delivering everything asked of us. Our partners are the best that the darker side has in professional services. Take a moment to consider some of our most popular offerings:

» Malaise of various and sundry forms
» Spiritual decay and early demise
» Transmutation. Lizards are our specialty
» Lassitude and Gender Reversal
» Portfolio Failure and 401(K) evaporations
» Amorous rejection and unlikely coupling
» Uncontrollable flatulence
» Warts

New offering for politicians...Speaking the Truth

Please also ask about our domestic programs with special rates for Royalty and other easily mutable forms of life.

~

Our rates are very competitive and only occasionally involve loss of life or actual soul. We are fully insured and charge only a minimum if our service fails to achieve the desired result.

"I asked for my rival company to become the target of a takeover and sure enough they were bought by a chain of Australian newspapers; thank you Dunsinane!"

Reginald Smallnuts
A former magazine owner

"Now that my elder Brother has become a Chihuahua my life is reaching its full potential, thanks to Dunsinane!"

Johnny Doomed
A very small business owner

~

Dunsinane Associates

Dastard Ragwold
Magister

Faustia Grillheart
Transmutrix

» Everywhere You Are «

Telephone: Birnamwood 3
E-Mail: newhags@scotsblood.net

Nap Time

Now and then
I take a nap
A nap on the couch
It's that or pretend I am paying attention.
To accelerate a reluctant somnolence
I return to another house
A house very far away
And in the past
Where my mother is busy in the kitchen.
While I doze off my jet lag in the closet she calls a
    bedroom
The almost rhythmic sounds of her kitchen are a
    sleeping draught
A draught so powerful no opiate competes.
I wonder now if she knew.

I Got This Body

I got this body from some people I knew,
For a while, at least,
And all of its shortcomings
Including shortness
Were presaged, previewed and
More than adequately demonstrated
Over the years we lived together.
But I ignored that, listening
Rather to their voices
Which illustrated another prophesy less physical
And am now stunned to welcome
Both my Mother and Father
In the shaving mirror every day.

Not My Barbecue

Everything has a price and good product functionality is one of those things. Nobody should expect perfection from anything. But one can expect a minimum. This is not the case with a certain spherical type of barbecue grill.

Imagine you were going to design a barbecue grill, what are the minimum features and functions you would include? How about these?

1. Easy ash disposal

2. Insulated lid handle

3. Insulated vent handle.

4. Insulated body handle

5. Lid with a hinge

6. Wheels that are large enough to roll

And here are a few features I would add for the premium model.

1. Hangers for utensils

2. Variable height grill

3. Electric lighter

You won't find any of these on a certain well-known brand of barbecue grills. I have one (it was a gift) and let me escort you through a typical experience you may have with it.

I keep my unit in the corner of my patio. You will have to move it to the middle, but the wheels are too small and it will not roll smoothly. Not helped by the short handle on the bowl which allows no leverage for stability and the awkward leg with no wheels which stubs easily on the patio. On a few occasions it has actually tipped over. Not the ash removal method I enjoy. Next ... remove the lid to recharge with fresh charcoal. I say remove instead of lift because with this model one has to actually remove the lid and lay it down somewhere. A nuisance when it is cold, dangerous when it is hot. It does have a short hook somewhere inside the lip but it is too short and damned hard to find when you are concentrating on cooking.

Let's say you forgot to empty the ash pan from the last cookout.

Bending down under the curve of the bowl making sure you don't bang your head on it you will now have to loosen three separate uncooperative small metal clips and then carefully inch the flimsy ash filled pan out from between the legs of the unit. Unless you are particularly dexterous you will inevitably spill some of the ash. If you are like me with moderate gifts you will spill more and from time to time drop the whole thing on the patio. And then of course, assuming you have now disposed of the ash, or swept it off somewhere, you must wrestle the dish back between the legs and reposition the thin painfully awkward clips to hold it more or less horizontally.

So now you have the unit in the middle of the patio with the lid off and the ash pan empty. Time to recharge with fresh charcoal. But alas when you glance into the bowl you see that even though you emptied the ash pan you forgot to 'riddle' the ash and fragments of charcoal still resting in the bottom of the bowl. To do this you must once again lean over and find the uninsulated metal combination vent and riddling lever. This lever must be wiggled back and forth so as to move three thin aluminum blades across the bottom of the bowl and with an amazing inefficiency push the ash and bits over three vent holes in the bottom of the bowl where they will then fall onto the flimsy ash pan or your patio if you forgot to put it back. As you move the lever back and forth you cannot see the inside of the bowl because you are bent over with your head once again banging the bowl and so it is impossible to know if you are actually moving the blades across the holes or just back and forth over the metal and pushing ash to and fro. You cannot see this lever easily from above. It takes quite a few oscillations of the lever to get any amount of ash to fall through the holes. And by the way the uninsulated lever can get rather hot after a grilling, so wear a glove. Not only that but if your unit is old the lever axle may have become rusted and hard to move so that when you do finally get it free you move the whole unit and risk tipping it over again.

Now you can charge the unit, but not until you have removed the grill itself from the bowl. It rests on small shelves projecting from the sides of the bowl. It has no hook whereby you could hang it on the side of the bowl while you fill the grate and so it too must rest on the ground.

"How's your back so far?"

Now you can really drop in as many charcoal briquettes as you wish. Finally, action! Squirt on the lighter fluid, drop the match and let her rip! Oops! Make sure you have opened the holes in the bottom of the bowl to let air flow in using the almost invisible lever. Did you bang your head again?

Ten or fifteen minutes pass and we have a nice pile of glowing coals on the grate. Now you can replace the grill and let the fire burn off the crud from last week's 'debacle de cuisine al fresco'.

Time to bring out whatever it is you are going to attempt to cook. Let's say it is steak. Are you going to grill it or barbecue? Grill? OK, you need to add more coals because the fire is really too far down to grill anything but seafood. So take off the grill… oops! ouch! Remember your glove! And place it on the patio. Warn the kids not to touch it. Folks with wooden decks need to have somewhere else to rest this piece of steel at several hundred degrees centigrade unless they would like a facsimile of the grill burnt into the deck. Remember there is no hanger for the grill.

Now, the manufacturer's manual suggests you can easily add more coals through the gaps in the grill next to the handles. Go ahead try that. The new coals will sit stubbornly at the edge of the others and refuse to join their brethren. Sure you can poke them into the center with something fireproof. Remember to use your glove!

O.K. The new coals are burning nicely and you can put the grill back in the bowl, but first you need to spread them out evenly, before you once more replace the grill. Remember your glove! Did I mention that there are two handles on the grill but of course they are too small, uninsulated and very hot.

Now … the big moment. You place the steaks on the grill, grasp your beverage, and assume a manly pose. Sadly the fire seems to have dwindled somewhat and your steaks do not sizzle. Aha! The vent holes under the bowl are not completely open! Bend down trying not to bang your head and move the lever one way or the other hoping that you are actually opening the aperture and not closing it. Have a guest guide you and yes, remember to use your glove!

"How's your back so far?"

Wonderful! Your steaks are now sizzling nicely and you can reassume your manly pose and make knowledgeable statements about cooking meat in the open. Minutes later depending on your guest's desire for rare or incinerated protein you have proven that you can master the beast.

But wait ... a guest has bought some marinated protein that requires not grilling but barbecuing. No problem. Once again remove the grill, with glove, to a safe place, and move the still burning coals into two colonies opposite each other on the grate, as the manufacturer's manual suggests.

This would be a good time to add a few more briquettes. Now replace the grill, and the so far unused lid! The idea here is to create an outdoor oven a.k.a. barbecue. On my model there is no thermometer to tell me what the temperature in the sphere has reached and so you would have to have another beverage until you trust it has got to an acceptable heat.

You give it half a beverage of time and lift the lid, remembering to use your glove, and, horrors! The coals are almost extinguished. Right ... you forgot to open the small wheel of vents on the lid which would allow a steady stream of refreshing air to feed you coals. OK easy fix. You replace the lid and adjust the lid vents to full open. You actually remember again to use your glove just in case the wretched thing is hot. Never fear it will be later.

Time for another beverage? Of course! And "How's your back so far?"

Now the whole assembly is hot enough for your guest to place their protein on the grill and you carefully lift and replace the lid. But ... ouch! The lid is now also damn hot and the dinky little handle is not well insulated and equally cauterizing.

Your reputation as chef is not yet so damaged and you make jokes about your days as a waiter in New York City where first and second degree burns were considered to be part of the 'shtick de cuisine.'

After another close to frozen beverage everyone suddenly recalls the 'barbecue' and you now automatically don your glove to lift the lid and hopefully find the almost invisible hook to safely hang the now radiant hemisphere of steel without burning yourself, anyone or anything else.

Luckily your guest's protein improved by its time in the sphere and the event resumes an even course. It might even be pleasant.

But on the patio is now a slowly cooling sphere of metal containing a lot of ash needing disposal and moving back into the far corner of the patio. A poorly designed and dangerous piece of equipment that somehow seems to have entranced Americans as a useful and efficient item when the truth is quite the reverse.

I know we can do better, the Chinese can make it cheaply and our backs and heads will thank us.

First Kiss

*A fragment illustrating the possible dangers of word
    prompts to poets.*
Prompts: Corn, evening, sandwich

It was about six in the evening
Six in the evening when juvenile lust is tumescent
When Anne McKilroy made her lips available to mine
In the back of the choir outing charabanc
She did not mind the smell of corn beef
Lingering from my lunch time sandwich

Freeway Backup

There's stasis on the freeway
A backup from the bridge
An accident in the tunnel
I left my lunch in the fridge

Grey cars with no lights
Vanish in the mist
A November Oregon morning
I remember that we kissed

The parking lot is crowded
The storm surges blow after blow
Two trucks block my progress
You'll miss me when I go?

I leave the car in limbo-land
I give a street kid a tip
There's a long walk to the office
Your taste lingered on my lip

Another dreary screen day
Click once here for madness
Scroll your life to hell
Did we really do our best?

I left my lunch in the fridge
I remember that we kissed
You'll miss me when I go
Your taste lingered on my lips
Did we really do our best?

Bob Sterry is a voice-over actor, audiobook narrator, writer, singer, occasional stage actor and humorist. Originally trained in England as a research analytical chemist, he immigrated into the United States in 1973 working as a wine waiter in New Jersey, a steel yard fork lift truck driver in Connecticut, before spending a professional career in the marketing of scientific instruments and services in New Jersey, Hong Kong and around the world.

It was not until he started writing short articles, essays and poetry in the 1990s that his creative talents found an outlet by reading his poetry at open mics. and singing seriously in choirs and extemporaneous groups. In 1999 he and his wife, Anne-Louise Sterry, a well-known speaker, singer and storyteller, founded a short lived but much loved faux cowboy wannabe band, 'Anne-Louise and the Cascade Urban Cowboys.' Discovering his on stage talent, he took the step to starting his own show of songs and spoken word. His singing is cabaret satire with Broadway and the English Musical Hall grinning in the wings with an occasional nod to the classical style. Recent shows were 'The Bob Sterry Atomic Summer Show' and 'The Book of Bob,' and 'A Sterry Sterry Night' with Anne-Louise Sterry. Bob also appeared in the Stumptown Stages productions of 'Ebenezer Ever after' and 'Jekyll and Hyde' and played Satan in Terry D. Kester's production of 'JB.'

Adding voice-over acting and audio-book narration were obvious steps, and thanks to voice coach Lesley Bailey and recording genius Marc Rose at FuseAudio Design, Bob offers his voice to anyone who needs it. Bob continues to write poetry and essays reflecting very much his cabaret style, with excursions into more serious commentary on life, humor and outright comedy. By the way, he is passionate about cycling, cooking, language and literature.